Pembrokeshire
a year and a day

Pembrokeshire
a year and a day

with an introduction by
John Archer-Thomson

Logaston Press

LOGASTON PRESS
Little Logaston Woonton Almeley
Herefordshire HR3 6QH
logastonpress.co.uk

First published by Logaston Press 2007
Copyright © Introduction, John Archer-Thomson 2007
Copyright © Photographs, as per photographer credited 2007

ISBN (paperback) 978 1 904396 72 7
(hardback) 978 1 904396 73 4

Hardback copy number: (of 500 copies)

Typeset by Logaston Press
and printed in Great Britain by
Bell & Bain Ltd., Glasgow

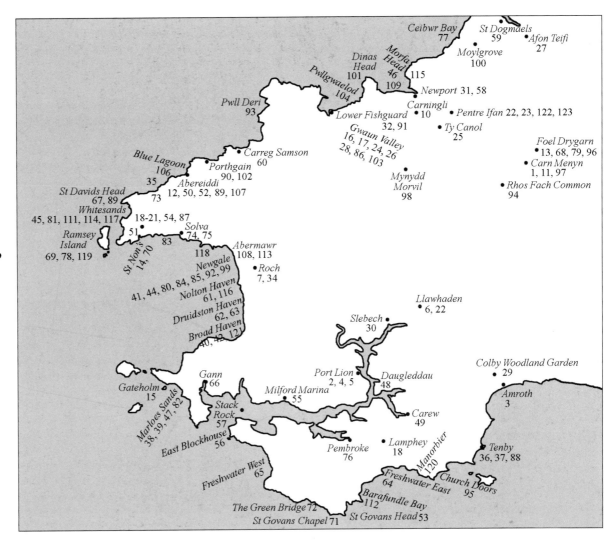

Map showing the locations of the images, the numbers equating to the page on which the image occurs

Ceibwr Bay 77
St Dogmaels 59
Afon Teifi 27
Moylgrove 100
Dinas Head 101
Morfa Head 46
115
109
Newport 31, 58
Pwllgwaelod 104
Carningli
Lower Fishguard 32, 91
Pentre Ifan 22, 23, 122, 123
Ty Canol 25
Pwll Deri 93
Gwaun Valley 16, 17, 24, 26 28, 86, 103
Foel Drygarn 13, 68, 79, 96
Carn Menyn 1, 11, 97
Carreg Samson 60
Mynydd Morvil 98
Rhos Fach Common 94
Blue Lagoon 106
Porthgain 90, 102
35
Abereiddi 12, 50, 52, 89, 107
St Davids Head 67, 89
73
Whitesands 45, 81, 111, 114, 117
18-21, 54, 87
Solva 74, 75
Ramsey Island 69, 78, 119
51
83
St Non's 14, 70
118
Abermawr 108, 113
Newgale 41, 44, 80, 84, 85, 92, 99
Roch 7, 34
Nolton Haven 61, 116
Llawhaden 6, 22
Druidston Haven 62, 63
Slebech 30
Broad Haven 40, 42, 121
Port Lion 2, 4, 5
Daugleddau 48
Colby Woodland Garden 29
Gann 66
Milford Marina 55
Gateholm 15
Carew 49
Amroth 3
Marloes Sands 38, 39, 47, 82
Stack Rock 57
Lamphey 18
Pembroke 76
Manorbier 120
Tenby 36, 37, 88
East Blockhouse 56
Freshwater West 65
Freshwater East 64
Church Doors 95
The Green Bridge 72
Barafundle Bay 112
St Govans Chapel 71
St Govans Head 53

Acknowledgments

I would like to thank all the photographers involved in the production of this book for their commitment to working in a co-operative manner and for the resulting pleasurable way in which the project has come to fruition.

In particular I would like to thank Eve Perloff for her thoughts and input into the design, and on behalf of Gary Roberts to give thanks to Tim Cripps for his aeroplane and being pilot whilst Gary added to his photographic collection.

Andy Johnson
Logaston Press

Preface

Whatever your vantage — from the Coast Path, a Preseli high top, from a boat on the Daugleddau, from one of the ribbon of islands — you will certainly appreciate that Pembrokeshire is a really special place. It is easy to see why, back in 1952, this was one of the first National Parks to be designated in Britain. This county has some of the finest coastal scenery in Europe — well befitting its National Park crown.

Like the others in the family of National Parks, the Pembrokeshire Coast is looked upon as one of Britain's 'breathing spaces' — places where people can get back in touch with their surroundings and what's important in life and breathe in the landscape.

Pembrokeshire is a small county, surrounded on three sides by the sea, and yet its landscape is so diverse, so impressive, so historic. There is evidence in abundance of man's influence upon the landscape through the millennia, shaping the scenery which we know and treasure today.

Artists through the centuries have captured the views, the shapes and forms of this treasured landscape and coastline and, in more recent generations, so too have the landscape photographers. Their skilled eye can give us an overall view of the landscape, drawing our attention to what is there to be seen within the 'eye of the beholder' for natural beauty.

But the real significance of the photographs is in the landscape as a whole; of one of the finest coasts in Europe more than half a century after the designation of the National Park. The Pembrokeshire Coast National Park is one of the smallest of the British parks, covering just 240 square miles (620 sq. km.) and is unusual in that much of its territory covers a long coastal strip. This stretches from Amroth in the south to St. Dogmaels, near Cardigan, in the north, all ribboned by the superb 186-mile (299 km.) Coast Path — one of Britain's 15 National Trails. In addition short boat trips take you to world-renowned bird islands.

The National Park does however also include the Preselis — magical uplands so much a part of British history and the source of Stonehenge's famous Bluestones — and the Daugleddau, the secluded tree-lined inner estuarine reaches around the fiord-like Haven Waterway.

Apart from the Coast Path there are around 500 miles of inland paths to enjoy too. Here the National Park Authority has always led the way in access and recreation — it was in Pembrokeshire that the concept of 'National Park guided walks' was originally pioneered and developed. This continues through the acclaimed Activities and Events programme which each year brings new delights, new insights on this special place to those who already love, or who grow to love, Pembrokeshire.

Office of the Pembrokeshire Coast National Park

The rare silver studded blue butterfly found in Pembrokeshire (Gary Llewellyn)

Introduction

This introduction covers three areas: geology; flora and fauna; and history as a background to the photographs that follow. In all three areas the word 'diversity' goes a long way: diversity of geology with rocks varying in age from a possible 650 million years old to a mere 20 million, with colour changes to match; diversity of landscape in the beaches, cliffs, estuaries, inlets, offshore islands, woodlands and the Preselis, with associated variety of habitat; and a long human history with a range of Neolithic monuments still standing and the added subsequent diversity of the mix of Welsh, Norman and English cultures and traditions.

Geology

Parts of Pembrokeshire are extremely old, with some rocks dating from the earliest period of the Earth's geological history, the Pre-Cambrian. To put this in context, the origin of the Earth is dated at 4.6 billion years in the past, the Pre-Cambrian dealing with all the events that occurred from then until a mere 570 million years ago when the Cambrian period is deemed to have commenced. The first 4 billion years were marked by extensive volcanic activity; any rocks created at the start of this period were probably reheated and thrown back into the mix. However, by some 3 billion years ago the Earth achieved solid status for the first time. Things had quietened down by the start of the Cambrian period, a time when Pembrokeshire was part of a large sag in the Earth's crust called a geo-syncline. This was filled by seawater and in this relatively quiet period material settled to the bottom of the geo-syncline to eventually produce a variety of beautifully coloured sedimentary rocks. At the same time early life forms were beginning to diversify, beginning the evolutionary process that eventually produced the millions of species that the Earth supports today. The large ocean that covered what was to become Pembrokeshire (and elsewhere) set the scene for the Ordovician and Silurian periods with further deposition of material in the ocean basin, but there were also periods of volcanic activity punctuating the peace and quiet. These volcanic bursts were particularly intense during the Ordovician, when massive layers of lava poured out of sub-marine volcanoes. As the cones grew, the craters emerged above the water and eruptions continued aerially.

The end of the Silurian period occurred approximately 400 million years ago and the Devonian began. At about this time in our Pembrokeshire story the North American tectonic plate (bringing a little bit of Scotland with it) ran up against the European plate creating the Caledonian mountains; outliers of this range of hills are visible in the Pembrokeshire landscape today at Cemaes Head.

In Devonian times things were radically different from the preceding 270 million years. The geo-syncline was replaced with a large mountain range to the north of Pembrokeshire and torrential streams flowed southwards away from these mountains, carrying an array of material towards the Dale area where the streams flowed into a delta system surrounded by desert. These Devonian rivers carried their sediment load into a sea whose coastline ran approximately east/west from the Bristol Channel to southern Ireland. In the desert environment the iron in the sediment was oxidised which has given the subsequent Old Red Sandstone its classic red colouration (pages 51, 53). Present day marine erosion strips iron off progressively smaller rock particles eventually leaving a silica grain behind which is golden in colour. Hence red cliffs yield golden sandy beaches given enough time.

By the time the Carboniferous period was reached (350 million years ago) the scenery had changed again. Shallow tropical seas teemed with life and ultimately gave rise to many famous fossils. A modern day equivalent would be Australia's Great Barrier Reef. South Pembrokeshire's limestone cliffs are the most notable results from this time; perhaps the best example of limestone scenery is the Green Bridge of Wales on the Castlemartin peninsula (page 72).

Conditions changed again 320 million years ago. The shallow limestone sea was uplifted sufficiently to transform it into a delta system once more. On this occasion, instead of limestone we find Millstone Grit and Coal Measures. Millstone Grits are a varied collection of rock associated with flowing freshwater (conglomerates, grit stones, sandstones and mudstones). Coal

Measures in Pembrokeshire were a rather thin and fragmented affair (and not as the name suggests all coal) but on the up side they were rich in particularly high quality anthracite. Coal Measure times were characterised by a depositional environment of semi-tropical swamps and fluctuating sea levels.

To finish Pembrokeshire's geological history, the African tectonic plate trundled up from the south and collided with Europe to form the Armorican mountains. (Indeed, not to be left out, all the world's current continents took this opportunity to have a massive reunion and formed a super-continent called Pangaea.) One of the most spectacular results of the Armorican (Hercynian) earth movements can be seen on the Dale Peninsula, near St. Ann's Head. This feature goes under the rather unfortunate name of 'Cobbler's Hole' and shows a series of folds next door to each other, with a fault zone running down through the exposed face.

Since that time the sea level has risen and fallen, Pangaea has split up and continents continue to move about the planet's surface. Any rocks that formed in Pembrokeshire during this time have been removed again, for the last 225 million years have been mainly about erosion, any period of stable sea level producing a 'sea floor', three of them standing at roughly 60m, 120m and 180m above present sea level.

There is one other process that must be mentioned, however, as its work is to be seen all over Pembrokeshire: that of glaciation. The last couple of million years have seen several ice ages. Whether we are currently in a warm period of the last ice age or at the end of that chapter of events is hotly debated. Ice has a massive effect on the landscape and at the coldest point of the ice age before last there was thought to be a two-mile thickness of ice over the top of the Preselis. When ice moves it carries debris with it and over some impressive distances. In Pembrokeshire there are glacial 'erratics' — stones and rocks carried by a glacier to a point far from their rock source — that came from the Hebrides. Meanwhile the glaciers scratched and scoured the land, creating valleys in weak areas stressed by earth movements millions of years before (such as the Gwaun Valley, see pages 16, 17, 103).

Flora and fauna

The best time of year for flowers on the Pembrokeshire coast is late May to early June. Although cliff-tops are a prime habitat they are only one of many different floral communities to see, for once again diversity comes to the fore. Because the county is host to many rock types there are also many different types of soil, which in turn favours floral diversity. Apart from the cliffs there are sand dunes, salt marshes, meadows, woodlands, freshwater marshes, bogs, river banks and coastal heath to name a few. Superimposed on the community diversity is another variant. Exposure to salt-laden wind can change the appearance and size of some plants so much that it can be difficult to recognize the same species in different locations. Location also has a big part to play on flowering time: bluebells on Skomer often flower two to three weeks later than their mainland counterparts, whilst thrift on salt marshes flowers after its coastal cousin by a similar margin.

Mention must also be made of lichens. On the coast lichens occupy the splash zone at the top of the shore, where it is too dry for marine organisms but too salt-sprayed for land plants. On shores sheltered from Atlantic breakers wave action is minimal so the splash zone is small, here land plants, including trees up the sheltered Daugleddau estuary, can grow just above high water mark. Exposed shores on the other hand receive the full force of Atlantic gales and salt spray is thrown many hundreds of metres up and over the cliffs. Consequently terrestrial vegetation retreats away from the tidal zone and the splash zone, now dominated by lichens, spreads 60 metres or more up the cliff.

Perhaps the most impressive faunal display is in the colonies of seabirds on the offshore islands and rock stacks. Puffins, guillemots and razorbills represent the auk family. Fulmars are relatively recent visitors having only bred in Pembrokeshire since 1949. Manx shearwaters are one of our rarest birds; Skomer and Skokholm islands may host something approaching 50% of the world's population. Inevitably there are gulls: herring, lesser and great black-backed help to make the auks' lives less pleasant. Kittiwakes save the gulls from disgrace, these are proper seagulls making a living perfectly respectably by feeding on plankton and surface fish that they have the decency to catch themselves, and this species does spend most of its life on or over the ocean. Then there are gannets, whose 180cm wingspan is the largest of any British seabird. Gannets plunge diving for fish is a sight to behold.

Choughs, a rare member of the crow family, are a familiar sight and sound along parts of the coastal strip. Their unique call makes chough spotting much easier as you invariably hear them long before seeing them, but although they advertise their presence by shouting at you they are very shy birds. Other members of the crow family include rooks (usually in groups), crows (often solitary), jackdaws (invariably up to no good) and ravens (recognizable by their deep croak and spectacular tumbling acrobatics).

Birds of prey, represented most obviously by buzzards, but also including kestrels, peregrine falcons and if you are lucky on Skomer the short-eared owl, are always exciting to see.

There are also lots of little brown jobs loitering in the bushes, trees and water margins. A favourite is the wheatear; not only does it pose for you (at least to look at through binoculars) but its name is a polite derivation of 'white-arse', based on the flash of white on the bird's rump that is revealed when it takes off.

Pembrokeshire's Atlantic grey seals number approximately 5,000 individuals and this is the largest population in southern Britain. They are resident all year round to a varying degree (in contrast to the seabird populations which are mostly gone by August, gannets excepting) and they have their pups in the autumn.

Out at sea you may be lucky enough to get a close encounter with some of the following: basking sharks and sunfish (July/ August), dolphins and porpoises (spring and autumn being the favourite periods), turtles (a large leatherback was encountered by the Skomer ferry in May 2004), and Risso's dolphins (once only in twenty years admittedly).

Just exploring the county can bring encounters with wildlife. Foxes and badgers can be seen going about their business late at night although daylight encounters are not impossible. Otters are present up the Cleddau estuary, and they are often encountered at Bosherston lily ponds. A reliable witness saw an otter washing the salt out of its fur (they often go sea fishing) in an irrigation pond on the Dale peninsula.

There are an estimated 56 native species of butterfly in the UK and Pembrokeshire has records for about 42 of these making it a good county for the lepidopterist. Peacock, red admiral, meadow brown, wall, speckled wood, various whites and the common blue (Britain and Ireland's most widespread) butterflies are often company for the coastal path walker and Pembrokeshire's diversity of habitats boost the total number of species encountered, with woodland, grassland, wetland and heath specialists. Some are rare: the silver studded blue, a heathland specialist whose range is in decline and is now a Biodiversity Action Plan species, has been recorded in the south of the county.

Beaches are another gem in Pembrokeshire's treasure chest. There are rocks, pools, sand patterns, plants and a host of animals to observe. Most rocky shore creatures sit there nicely for you, it's the most sedate type of safari there is.

Below the low tide mark Pembrokeshire continues to be beautiful and interesting. The sea around Skomer Island is Wales' only (and the UK's second) official Marine Nature Reserve (MNR) managed by the Countryside Council for Wales (CCW).

History

At the end of the last Ice Age, some 12,000 years ago, sea level would have been about 100m lower than today. Late Palaeolithic man would have lived (temporarily) in caves at the base of the present cliffs from where they would have hunted the like of Woolly Mammoth on what is now the seabed.

From around 10,000 years ago the climate started to improve. Warming must have been gradual, perhaps not even noticeable over a human lifetime (only about 30 years in those days). As the climate changed so did the prey that humans hunted; woolly mammoth and cave bear gave way to reindeer and horse. There is evidence that (true to later form) humans were soon severely depleting big game populations and had to look around for other sources of nourishment. Rocky shores were exploited for limpets, and man also became more of a 'gatherer', as nuts and berries became a greater part of the diet for Mesolithic (or middle stone age) people. Flint was a valuable commodity at this time and a rare one in Pembrokeshire. Working this valuable resource was a skilled business and scrapers, borers, arrowheads and spear points were all manufactured in a limited number of 'flint factories'. On the Dale peninsula near Castlebeach it is possible to find examples of worked flint from this period on the coastal footpath.

Around 5,000 years ago the practice of agriculture was adopted in Pembrokeshire, having spread from the Middle East. Until then people had been essentially nomadic hunter-gatherers, but with the advent of farming, lifestyles changed completely. Houses (hut circles) were built, a necessity if you had to remain in the area for crops to grow. Livestock were domesticated and their movements controlled with the erection of stone field boundaries. Perhaps the most famous relics from this new Stone Age (Neolithic) period are the burial chambers that still grace the landscape (pages 22, 23, 60, 122, 123). These marvellous megalithic (big-stone) structures are contemporary with the most famous one of them all, Stonehenge, and indeed the links are more than just temporal as spotted dolerite from the Preselis was used in the second phase of that monument.

Remains of the subsequent Bronze Age in Pembrokeshire are less obvious. Beaker Folk (makers of finely decorated urns) set out from Whitesands Bay (pages 81, 111, 114, 117) for trade routes with Ireland from about 3,500 years ago. Metals were the new flint. Copper from the Wicklow Mountains was mixed with Cornish tin to make bronze and later a trade in gold flourished. It was about this time that people first cremated their dead. Burial chambers were now out of date and little cairns became fashionable instead.

Once again new ideas gradually percolated into Pembrokeshire, this time concerning a new metal, iron. At the same time population was increasing, and perhaps not simply by growth of the local population but also from migration caused by a worsening climate and warfare in central Europe. The effect was to put pressure on local resources and heighten the possibility of conflict, as a result the most obvious Iron Age remains in Pembrokeshire are fortifications. In Pembrokeshire these were, in the main, formed by cutting ditches and forming banks across narrow cliff-top promontories, rather than by encircling a complete hill-top. Early versions had just the one bank but later versions had two banks, each bank being a spear's throw apart.

The end of the Iron Age is defined by the arrival of the Romans. Carmarthen seems to be the westernmost settlement substantiated by evidence; rumour suggests a settlement at Whitesands (called *Manapia*) but it has not been found. The Romans never dominated the Atlantic and upland areas of the British Isles in the way that they did lowland Britain. When the Roman legions left in 410 AD the Celts of the area were quite able to look after their own destiny, but much of the rest of the UK was thrown into the chaos known as the Dark Ages. Pembrokeshire meanwhile slid gracefully into the Age of the Saints.

No one has yet authoritatively dated the arrival of the Christian message in Pembrokeshire, but as the area was essentially untouched by Rome, it is most likely to have arrived from Ireland or Brittany, the sea then being the main thoroughfare, as indeed it was until quite recently. From about 400AD onwards the St. Davids peninsula was a focus for early Christian activity.

St. Non was the daughter of a high-ranking Welsh chieftain (named Cynir) who was not too delighted about his daughter's impending motherhood, as she was not married. In a reaction which might be considered extreme, especially as Prince Sant (of Ceredigion) had probably raped her, he decided to kill his daughter and her un-born child. St. Non fled but was caught wandering around the cliff-tops in a thunderstorm when she went into labour. Child-birth caused her to grip the rock so tightly that an imprint of her fingers is believed to remain to this day as is a healing well of crystal water, but she duly gave birth to St. David. This occurred in *c*.520. When an adult, David established a harshly ascetic community in Merry Vale (somewhat at variance with the rather cheerful name); apparently if St. David found himself thinking lewd thoughts he would go and immerse his body in the cold sea until he felt chaste again. St. Davids, as his establishment became known, grew in importance to the extent that by the Middle Ages two pilgrimages to St. Davids were worth one to Rome.

Nobody really knows who St. Govan was but the most popular idea is that he was Sir Gawaine, of round table fame, who turned hermit after the death of King Arthur. There are mysterious forces at work at St. Govan's Chapel. Apparently it is impossible to count the number of steps down to and up from the Chapel and arrive at the same number twice as the mind is clouded by the numinous quality of the area. It is thought that there was a chapel on the site maybe as early as the time of St. David, but the present structure dates from the thirteenth century and has been restored by the National Park Authority (see page 71).

Of the many tales of King Arthur, one has it that in this Age of the Saints he ruled the ancient kingdom of Dyfed until the age of ninety when he lost a battle and was beheaded near St. Davids.

In the eighth, ninth and tenth centuries Viking raiders sacked the coastline of Pembrokeshire many times. They must have seen St. Davids as a particular source of spoil, for despite it being hidden in a dip they found it eight times in as many decades. However other Vikings appear to have settled along the Milford Haven waterway which suggests a more peaceful relationship.

The Normans arrived in Pembrokeshire by 1090. They took for themselves the rich farmland in the southern half of Pembrokeshire based on a new lordship at Pembroke, and a defensive screen of castles was built from Roch (page 34) through Llawahden, Narberth, Carew (page 49) and Tenby to Amroth to keep the unruly Celts to the north at bay. It is interesting to reflect how Pembrokeshire was split into an 'Englishry' — the Norman dominated south — and a 'Welshry' — the Celtic dominated north — and how this reflects the geology. The ancient geological heartland of north Pembrokeshire has poorer soils; therefore it has never been farmed as intensively as the south. Thus geology and history have conspired to divide Pembrokeshire up in to a northern and southern province.

Pembroke Castle (page 76) dominates the western end of this excellent example of a Norman walled town. William Marshall started building the present structure in about 1190; work continued under the supervision of his five sons until it was largely completed by 1245. Although hopelessly out of date by contemporary military standards, the castle suffered a seven-week siege at the hands of Oliver Cromwell himself during the Civil War.

St. Davids flourished after the Norman arrival, and as a result has the longest continuous story of any religious settlement in the UK at over 1,400 years. Chapels existed from early on but building on a large scale began in 1178 under Bishop Peter de Leia, continuing for the next 300 years to give the basic structure seen today (see pages 18–21). From 1328 Bishop Gower extensively remodelled and extended the buildings, and in 1509 Bishop Vaughan added a third tier to the tower. Henry VIII's time saw the buildings fall into a state of disrepair. John Nash restored the west front in 1793 (to a rather unenthusiastic reception). In 1862, the gothic revivalist, George Gilbert Scott effectively saved the cathedral with a massive renovation project, which he viewed as one of his greatest achievements.

Lamphey Palace was constructed as a rural retreat for the bishop in the early thirteenth century (page 18). Bishop Richard Carew, using high quality stonemasons from outside Pembrokeshire, added to the Palace in the latter years of the century. Bishop Gower undoubtedly gave the Palace its greatest splendour by adding a new hall and gatehouse and remodelling the courtyard. After the Reformation the palace passed from Church to State ownership; in Elizabethan times it was the home of the Devereux family.

The sea long remained the major highway for the county, with the seventeenth and eighteenth centuries featuring prominently in the lives of local ports. Solva (pages 74, 75), for example, has been a port since the 1300s. (It must surely have been host to Neolithic coracles long before that). It had the advantage over its neighbour, Porth Clais, in that it was deeper and able to accommodate ships of up to 300 tons. Solva's importance grew in the eighteenth century with cargoes of coal, wood, grain, butter and woven goods destined for Wexford, Bristol and further afield. The port was also the main lime-burning centre for the St. Davids peninsula, boasting ten working kilns in Victorian times, many of which are still visible on the east side of the harbour. The main street, now a colourful haven for visitors, would have been a pretty messy affair with warehouses, mills, stables, blacksmiths, wheelwrights, carpenters, saddlers and weavers all jostling for trade.

Newport (page 58) is the first major inlet and one of the best beaches on the North Pembrokeshire coast. By the mid 1500s the quay at Parrog (page 109) was a trading post linked with ports up the Bristol Channel exporting wool and slate, importing coal and limestone; all vessels had to negotiate the hazardous sandbar that attempts to block the estuary and gives

lifeboat crews a run for their money. Newport, along with Fishguard and Lawrenny, boasted a proper shipyard, but there were thirty or so other small scale boat-building sites around the coast.

Other nautical endeavours of a slightly more suspect nature also flourished locally, namely 'wrecking' and piracy. Wreckers would light false lights on treacherous stretches of shore to lure hapless vessels onto the rocks and then plunder the cargo. Pembrokeshire's most famous pirate was Bartholomew Roberts, born in Little Newcastle in 1682. He turned to piracy in 1719 and took on the rather more convincing name of 'Black Bart'. In a brief (three year) but impressive career he captured 400 ships to earn his reputation as the terror of the Spanish Main.

In 1797 the French invaded near Fishguard under the (rather reluctant) leadership of an American by the name of Tate. A disorderly invading force deteriorated further on the discovery that most of the local farms were well stocked with wine from a recently wrecked Portuguese vessel. Surrounded by drunken officers and soldiers, Tate surrendered to the rather fortunate Lord Cawdor whose battle skills were rather stronger in the realms of theory than they were in practice. In the meantime, a local heroine, one Jemima Nicholas, a tall, stout Amazon of a woman working as a cobbler in Fishguard, reputedly marched out with a pitchfork, captured twelve Frenchmen in a field near Llanwnda, locked them up and went out to capture more.

The sea remained important to Pembrokeshire, and in the 1800s there were even floating village shops; ships from

Bristol would sell to local villages like Solva, Porthclais and Lower Fishguard before heading back up the Bristol Channel to restock. Larger vessels made it to places as far afield as Newfoundland (for building timber), Chile (for phosphates/guano) and Morocco (for corn). Coastal villages in Pembrokeshire were in more direct and constant contact with each other than they were with their respective hinterlands. But the railway changed everything. Trade routes shifted away from the coast and the subsequent advent of metalled roads and lorries killed many coastal villages stone dead. A tradition dating back to the Neolithic had run its course and coastal Pembrokeshire became isolated. Many rather forlorn remnants of what used to be thriving ports can be seen along the coast today, Porthgain (pages 90, 102) is a classic example, but the news is not all bad. Isolation from human activity means that natural history maintains a stronghold.

Even before the arrival of the railways, there had been industrial enterprises in Pembrokeshire. Abereiddi slate quarry (pages 50, 52), for example, operational from about 1830 to 1904, produced rather poor quality slates which were taken by tramway to Porthgain for shipment. When quarrying ceased, an opening to the sea was created and the area flooded to create the present day Blue Lagoon (page 106). Divers favour this sheltered water body on windy days as a safer, calmer alternative to the open ocean. The function of the tower overlooking the Blue Lagoon is disputed but the best explanation is that the manager's wives used it as a tearoom. The coastal cottages and buildings were abandoned after a combination of a typhoid epidemic and the great storm of 1938.

During the nineteenth century substantial investment in the new towns of Milford, Neyland and Pembroke Dock meant that the Haven became a harbour of great strategic importance; consequentially plans were put forward to fortify the waterway properly for the first time. Initially attention was focused around the Royal Naval Dockyard at Pembroke Dock (reckoned during its heyday in the nineteenth century to be the most advanced shipyard in the world), but fortifications soon spread seaward until in total the defences could accommodate 1,900 men and 220 heavy guns (see page 56, 57).

Milford Haven's history is one of a series of false starts. It started out in 1810 as a Quaker Nantucket whaling station, but that proved unsuccessful. It was nearly a great trans-Atlantic terminus. It was nearly a world-class naval dockyard. It was nearly a great fishing port, indeed once it was possible to walk from one side of the docks to the other on the decks of the local fishing fleet.

In Milford's ultimate favour, though, was the fact that it was a natural deep-water harbour. When the oil industry was looking for a port to accommodate 100,000-ton tankers, Milford seemed the obvious choice. Esso built the first oil refinery in 1958 and BP added a storage facility on the opposite shore. Texaco, Gulf and Amoco followed suit but the promise for local employment was never realised as fully as hoped, the companies bringing a lot of their own trained personnel with them. Now Esso and BP have gone. Many of the other companies have changed their names or indeed their products. The most recent development is the storage of Liquefied Natural Gas at the former Gulf site.

Activities

Pembrokeshire has a lot of potential for outdoor activities. On land, walking and cycling are well catered for and for those of a more adventurous nature there is rock climbing. Early season climbing is feasible as the steep rocks dry quickly and many act as sun traps, especially the internationally famous, good quality limestone pitches in the south of the county from The Green Bridge of Wales eastwards. The north also boasts some superb sea climbing on short slabs or walls from Solva round to, and including, St. Davids Head (page 51).

On the sea, sailing, boating, kayaking and scuba diving bring visitors from all over the UK and further afield. Surfing here can be very good as many of the beaches have unobstructed access to Atlantic breakers (pages 42, 43). Freshwater West is well known as the most consistent surfing beach in Wales with wave amplitudes often two feet bigger than neighbouring sites. Newgale (pages 41, 80, 84, 85) is perhaps the most accessible beach in the whole county and although it faces south-west it does get some lee courtesy of the Marloes peninsula. Westdale, Barafundle (page 112) and Tenby South beaches all have their devotees and it depends on the weather as to which is favoured on a particular day.

Photographic lighting

Photography literally means writing with light and, all other things being equal, the better the pen (quality of light) the better the essay (photograph). Landscape photographers often talk about the golden two hours after sunrise and similarly before sunset. Some photographers go as far as to say never use a camera after 10am and before 4pm. There is no doubt that the quality of light can be at its best at the edges of the day but there are (as with all photographic rules) exceptions. Winter days may be good throughout as the sun is permanently low in the sky. Strong daylight in the summer may favour bold, simple compositions with rich colouration. Misty days, days with high, thin cloud and even rainy days all have merit for different photographic themes. Shooting with the light behind, and slightly to one side of, the camera favours many subjects, but picture taking straight into the sun can yield spectacular, dramatic, different results.

Thus, many of the photographs in this book are taken in the early morning or at dusk, which has given rise to the layout adopted: looking at Pembrokeshire over the course of a day that also spans the seasons. Hence the title: Pembrokeshire: a year and a day.

Carn Menyn, the Preselis (Jeremy Moore)

Early morning winter or spring light is truly magical. There is no better time of day or year to take a photograph (David Wilson)

Amroth. The rising spring sun bathes the beach in a warm glow (David Wilson)

The sun rising to the right and a snow cloud to the left — a photograph of true contrasts (David Wilson)

The river near my home is one of my favourite locations. On mornings like this you can see why (David Wilson)

Llawhaden. Not long after sunrise on a beautiful May morning. The mist-shrouded trees add a hint of mystery (David Wilson)

A misty start near Roch Castle — the harbinger of another lovely day (Gary Roberts)

Carn Llidi and (nearest camera) Pen Berri, with St Davids Head to the far right (Gary Roberts)

St Davids Head and Pwll Deri during sea fog (Jeremy Moore)

The Preselis from Carningli with Cilgwyn and Carnedd Meibion Owen in the foreground (Betty Rackham)

Frost on the Preselis. Taken near Mynachlogddu, with Carn Menyn in the background (Eric Lees)

First light near Abereiddi on the north coast of Pembrokeshire with Pen Berri across the bay — and Carn Llidi in the distance (Gary Roberts)

Early Morning, the Preselis. Captured soon after dawn from the top of Foel Drygarn, looking towards Carningli and Newport (Eric Lees)

St Non's Chapel near where Non reputedly gave birth to David (c.500). This building dates from the 1930s (Richard Hellon)

Gateholm. The quartz grains glow in the early morning light (John Archer-Thomson)

Cwm Gwaun at Llanerch, a quiet and beautiful valley winding from the Preselis to Fishguard (Tony Rackham)

Ramsons at Tregynon. In the spring the woods in Cwm Gwaun are full of bluebells and ramsons (Tony Rackham)

Lamphey Bishop's Palace, east of Pembroke. Long shadows cast by early morning sunlight reveal delicate details of the window tracery of this medieval ruin (Toby Driver, Crown Copyright RCAHMW)

(Far right) St Davids Cathedral. In the spring the bluebells emerge just before the leaves of the limes; timing is everything (Richard Hellon)

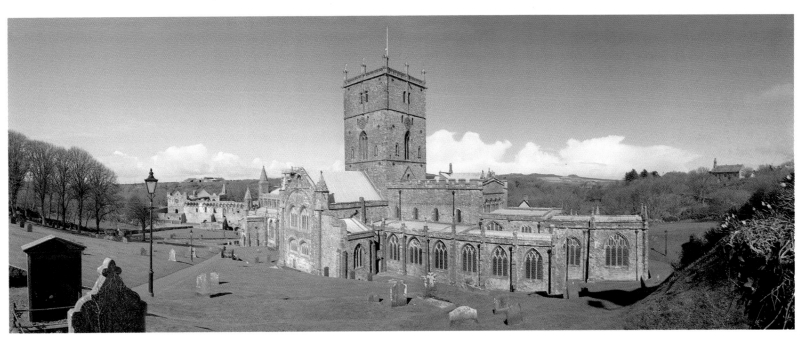

St Davids in its incomparable valley setting in early spring. The ruined Bishop's Palace is on the left (Richard Hellon)

On winter evenings in the Cathedral nave very little light comes from the windows, but the built-in illumination dramatically picks out the rood and the organ screen (Richard Hellon)

*(Far right)
The south quire aisle in St Davids Cathedral from the south transept (Richard Hellon)*

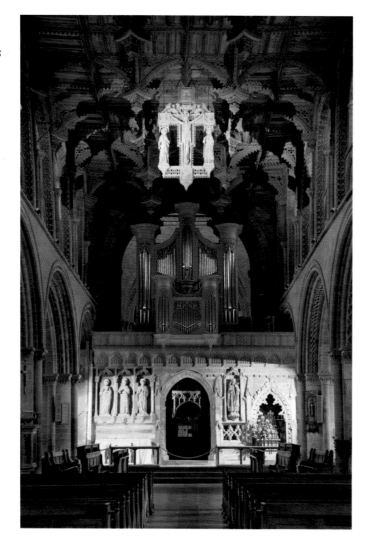

20

The colourful wooden panelling beneath the tower of the Cathedral (Richard Hellon)

Gelli Camp Iron Age fort, Llawhaden. Tractor lines in spring grassland weave intricate patterns around the circular earthwork of this pre-historic defended farmstead (Toby Driver, Crown Copyright RCAHMW)

(Far right) Pentre Ifan Neolithic burial chamber. The gaunt stone chamber, first erected 6,000 years ago, casts long shadows over the remains of the elongated long mound behind (Toby Driver, Crown Copyright RCAHMW)

Pentre Ifan Cromlech with Carningli in the background (Eric Lees)

Near the Gwaun Valley on a spring evening. The two lines of trees crossing the field perhaps show the line of an old track (Richard Hellon)

Woodland Edge, Ty Canol Wood. On the slopes of the Preselis, to the rear of Newport (Eric Lees)

In the ancient woods near Pontfaen some trees fall but they do not die (Richard Hellon)

The Afon Teifi Gorge near Cilgerran around midday (Eric Lees)

Bluebell Pathway, Coed Gelli Fawr. Spring arrives in Cwm Gwaun (Betty Rackham)

Colby Woodland Garden. A spring photograph (Eric Lees)

Bluebell time in the private grounds of Slebech Park Woods on the banks of the River Cleddau (Gary Roberts)

Spring flowers on the coast path leading to the Parrog, Newport. Thrift, trefoil and squills form a coloured carpet (Betty Rackham)

Fishguard Old Harbour (Eric Lees)

Nevern Estuary, Newport (Gary Llewellyn)

Roch Castle — the Norman fortress in all its majesty on this glorious summer's day. It is still in private hands — and not open to visitors — but you can rent it for your holiday! (Gary Roberts)

North Pembrokeshire with Porthgain in the foreground, Carn Llidi and St Davids Head beyond (Toby Driver, Crown Copyright RCAHMW)

Tenby Harbour (Eric Lees)

Tenby. A view across the colourful terraces, streets and harbour from the south-east (Toby Driver, Crown Copyright RCAHMW)

Rock Pools at Marloes Sands. Late morning looking in the opposite direction to the shot opposite (Eric Lees)

Raggle Rocks, Marloes Sands. The far end of the beach during mid morning early summer (Eric Lees)

Waves breaking on Broad Haven beach, west Pembrokeshire (Toby Driver, Crown Copyright RCAHMW)

Newgale Beach (Jeremy Moore)

This wave is often called 'the wedge'. A surfer takes a closer look (Adrian Hawke)

A popular sport around the coastline. Here the surfer makes his own mark on the wave (Adrian Hawke)

Newgale: 'The Green Cathedral' — a surfing term (Gary Roberts)

Carreg Rhoson and North Bishop from Whitesands, St Davids (Jeremy Moore)

Rainbow over Morfa Head seen from the other side of Newport Bay (Tony Rackham)

*Above Marloes Beach on
a peerless July morning
(Gary Roberts)*

The confluence of the East and West branches of the River Cleddau at high tide (Gary Roberts)

The ancient and beautiful ruins of Carew Castle, on a tributary of the River Cleddau (Gary Roberts)

Abereiddi Quarry, taken in late afternoon with a telephoto lens (and polariser) gives an abstract feel (John Archer-Thomson)

Carreg-y-Barcud, a classic climbing area. This shot was taken whilst hanging on a rope halfway down the cliff (Adrian Hawke)

At the south end of Abereiddi beach is a vertical cliff of multicoloured slate. The pennywort was a bonus (Richard Hellon)

St Govans Head at high tide (Eric Lees)

St Davids Lifeboat Station, extending into the clear waters of Porthstinan (Toby Driver, Crown Copyright RCAHMW)

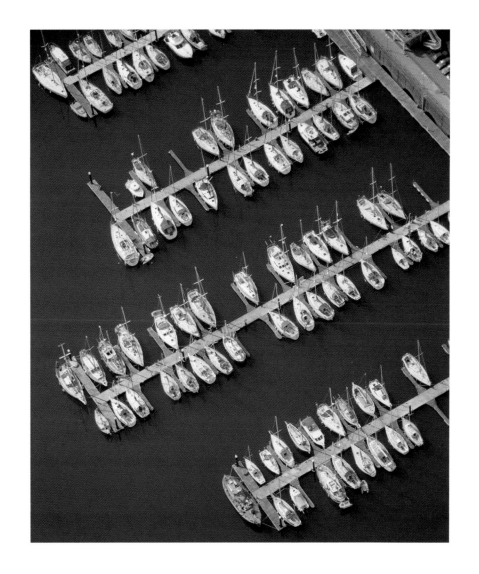

Rows of boats in Milford Marina (Toby Driver, Crown Copyright RCAHMW)

East Blockhouse Radar. This survivor from the Second World War overlooks the mouth of Milford Haven from treacherous cliffs, providing a forward defence for the gun batteries on East Blockhouse Point (Toby Driver, Crown Copyright RCAHMW)

Stack Rock Fort, an isolated gun battery commanding a rock in the middle of the Milford Haven waterway. The fort started life as a small trefoil-plan battery in 1852, still visible from the air within the fort, before being enveloped by the more massive, circular tower we see today (Toby Driver, Crown Copyright RCAHMW)

Nevern Estuary and the Parrog, Newport (Jeremy Moore)

The Teifi Estuary at St Dogmaels, looking across to Ceredigion (Jeremy Moore)

Carreg Samson, a Neolithic burial chamber, above Abercastle. Garn Fawr and Strumble Head lie across the bay (Gary Roberts)

Nolton Haven. After a low pressure has passed over, north-westerly winds bring clear skies and crisp light (Adrian Hawke)

Haroldston Chins, Druidston Haven (Gary Llewellyn)

Druidston, looking north (John Archer-Thomson)

Freshwater East. The late afternoon light perfectly illuminates the dappled sand and grasses in the foreground (David Wilson)

Freshwater West. Captured on a stormy afternoon, this is a dramatic photograph with extreme contrasts of tone (David Wilson)

Gann reflections, with rare absence of a coastal breeze to give a pristine reflective surface (John Archer-Thomson)

St. Davids Head Neolithic burial chamber with an amazing sky (polarised for maximum effect) (John Archer-Thomson)

Summer heather in the Preselis with Foel Drygarn in the background (Eric Lees)

St Davids Head from Ramsey Island (Jeremy Moore)

Storm at St Non's. With the waves at over 20ft, there's some good opportunity for some wild Pembrokeshire shots (Adrian Hawke)

St Govans Chapel (Gary Llewellyn)

The Green Bridge (John Archer-Thomson)

Near Abereiddi, with Penberry and Carn Llidi in the background (Jeremy Moore)

Solva. High view of the former fishing village and its inlet at low tide (Toby Driver, Crown Copyright RCAHMW)

Solva harbour which gains added protection from the bend in the inlet (Richard Hellon)

Pembroke Castle (Gary Roberts)

View north past Ceibwr Bay showing folds in the rock strata (Betty Rackham)

Ramsey Island from St Davids Head with erratics in the foreground brought by the last ice age (Richard Hellon)

Towards Foel Drygan, Preselis (Gary Llewellyn)

Newgale. As seen when approaching the beach from the road to St Davids (Eric Lees)

A ride at Whitesands Bay (Eric Lees)

The Beach, Marloes, at high tide (Jeremy Moore)

The northern coast of St Brides Bay, near St Davids (Jeremy Moore)

Newgale in the pale translucent light of winter. A colour shot but almost monochrome in aspect (Gary Roberts)

A solitary sand-yachtsman has Newgale to himself for once (Gary Roberts)

Frozen leaves, Pontfaen,
Gwaun Valley
(Gary Llewellyn)

Winter afternoon, St Davids. Mists rise around the Cathedral (Betty Rackham)

An alternative view of Tenby taken from Amroth. Moments later the shafts of winter light were gone (David Wilson)

The sun appeared fleetingly over Abereiddi on a bleak winter's day; I love the pattern formed by the white pine-ends (David Wilson)

Porthgain. This is one of many picturesque harbours that dot the Pembrokeshire coast (David Wilson)

Lower Fishguard (Gary Llewellyn)

A meteorological effect off Newgale known in photographic jargon as a 'GBH', a God-be-here (Gary Roberts)

Pwll Deri from Garn Fawr (Gary Llewellyn)

Rhos Fach Common. Taken on a freezing winter's day, the snow softens an otherwise dark brooding image (David Wilson)

Church Doors, Skrinkle Haven
(Gary Llewellyn)

Towards Foel Drygarn in the Preselis (John Archer-Thomson)

Carn Menyn, the Preselis (Jeremy Moore)

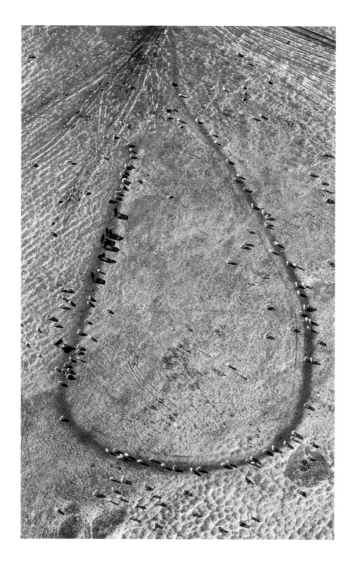

Patterns of winter livestock feeding on frosty pasture on Mynydd Morvil, north-west of New Inn in north Pembrokeshire (Toby Driver, Crown Copyright RCAHMW)

Snowy Pebbles, Newgale.
A rare view in Pembrokeshire
with a small window of light
(Adrian Hawke)

View from above Moylgrove looking out towards Strumble Head (Tony Rackham)

The Nevern Estuary seen from the Iron Bridge looking towards Dinas Head (Tony Rackham)

Porthgain Harbour (Gary Llewellyn)

River Gwaun, Pontfaen,
Gwaun Valley
(Gary Llewellyn)

Where Dinas Head joins the mainland are two bays, Cwm Yr Eglwys one side and Pwllgwaelod (above) the other (Tony Rackham)

Newgale Razorshell
(John Archer-Thomson)

The Blue Lagoon, the flooded quarry at Abereiddi, with a dramatic sky as the sun sets in the west (Adrian Hawke)

Abereiddi in the evening. A prominent headland recognised by its watch tower and distant views towards Ramsey (Adrian Hawke)

Evening tide Newgale. Pebbles, sand and waves, topped with sunshine, can make some evocative images (Adrian Hawke)

Bass fishing on incoming tide on the Afon Nyfer at The Parrog, showing Dinas Head in the background (Eric Lees)

Cat Rock, Newport, with Dinas Island in the background (Jeremy Moore)

Whitesands. Pembrokeshire can change quickly, overcast and wet all day, and then an opportunity (Adrian Hawke)

Barafundle (Gary Llewellyn)

Evening tide at Abermawr. A special moment as a wave splashes up in front of the sun (Adrian Hawke)

In midsummer the sun sets behind St Davids Head making the sea in Whitesands Bay glow (Richard Hellon)

Returning home Traeth Mawr, Newport. Seagulls, longboats and a lone yacht head for the Parrog (Betty Rackham)

Late fishing, Nolton. With the sun setting further south, autumn to spring is the time to visit this small beach (Adrian Hawke)

Whitesands, evening. Still in my wetsuit after a surf, this was a bit of a grab shot (Adrian Hawke)

I love the strength of Pointz Castle, the way it dominates the north end of St Brides Bay (Adrian Hawke)

*Late evening
over Ramsey
(Adrian Hawke)*

*Manorbier
(Gary Llewellyn)*

Emmet Rock,
Broad Haven
(Gary Llewellyn)

Pentre Ifan (David Wilson)

Pentre Ifan (Jeremy Moore)

Frameable prints of all the images in this book are available from
Celtic Images at Hilton Court Gardens
at Roch, Pembrokeshire (www.celticimages.co.uk)
or direct from the photographers themselves

The Photographers

John and Sally Archer-Thomson are a husband and wife team specialising in landscape and natural history photography. With a background and training in natural history and coastal ecology they have been photographing the landscapes, flora, fauna and underwater life of Pembrokeshire for over twenty years. They have a picture library (film and digital) of over 15,000 images including material from their travels in Nepal, India, China, Tibet, Africa, South America, New Zealand and the Caribbean. They can be contacted via email: jhsat@hotmail.com, or www.natural-inspiration.co.uk.

Dr Toby Driver FSA joined the Royal Commission on the Ancient and Historical Monuments of Wales in 1995. He undertakes aerial reconnaissance across Wales to discover and record archaeological sites and landscapes. His photographs are held in the National Monuments Record of Wales and can be consulted online at www.coflein.gov.uk. His book, *Pembrokeshire: Historic Landscapes from the Air*, was pubished by the Royal Commission in 2007.

Adrian Hawke's fine art landscapes have grown out of nearly twenty years of experience and illustrate how he sees the landscapes of Pembrokeshire. He aims to create images which stir emotions or memories and encapsulate mood and feeling. Different techniques are employed, but perhaps most impor-tant is timing; timing of light, seasons, weather and tide. This knowledge allows him to produce resonant images that make him one of Pembrokeshire's leading landscape photographers. (Phone: 07779531426; www.Adrianhawke.co.uk).

After retiring from a career in medical science, **Richard Hello**n moved to Pembrokeshire twenty-one years ago but only started taking photography seriously over the last seven years. He enjoys a wide variety of subjects, from landscapes through architecture to close-ups of flowers, lichens and rocks. The discipline of photography has served to increase his appreciation of the natural world. The range of his work can be seen on his web site (www.richardhellon.com). For further contact: richardhellon@aol.com or 01437 721168.

The ability to capture the simple majesty and beauty of Pembrokeshire in its natural state is the hallmark of **Eric Lees'** work. Early morning starts and evening trips from his home in Cilgerran ensure he shows the landscape in all its garments and through each season, bringing out the essence of the unique spirit inherent in this land and coastline.

Born in Pembrokeshire in 1978, photography has always been a passion of **Gary Llewellyn**. His uniquely stylized compositions are a representation of his love for perfection, which transports viewers into a dynamic, richly saturated and astonishing new world. He often harnesses the last glimmers of twilight within extremely long exposures and is constantly searching for 'perfect light and composition'. He has no formal training in photography having previously completed a Masters Degree in Environmental Education. To view his extensive portfolio please visit www.garyllewellyn.com.

Jeremy Moore is a landscape and outdoor photographer based in Aberystwyth with a foot in both the commercial and creative worlds. His 'Wild Wales / Cymru Wyllt' postcards and calendar are widely available, but he tackles other subject matter in more depth with a more documentary style. He continues to be inspired by the beauty of the Welsh landscape, and also explores our use and abuse of it in a visual sense. His book on Blaenau Ffestiniog was published in March 2007. For further information, see www.wild-wales.com

Betty Rackham FRPS has used a camera for most of her life, starting with a Box Brownie, and now works with digital cameras. After retiring as Head of Photography in a big F.E. college, she was glad to escape to Pembrokeshire and have time for her own work. She has always been fascinated by the way light and shadow can alter colours and enhance atmosphere. Pembrokeshire's varied landscape and constantly changing clear light means there is always something to photograph. (Phone: 01239 820068 or 01794 368498)

Tony Rackham FRPS obtained a fellowship of the Royal Photographic Society in 1986 and his work has been accepted in many open exhibitions. The images he produces seek to capture the beauty of natural subjects such as plants, animals and unspoilt landscapes. He finds Pembrokeshire a constant source of inspiration with its rich wildlife, its rugged coast and gentle mountains, its ever-changing weather and its beautiful light. (Phone: 01239 820068 or 01794 368498)

Gary Roberts was born in Pembrokeshire in 1941. After a career in engineering ranging from Concorde to domestic appliances and patenting and marketing his own designs worldwide, he returned to his homeland with his partner Ann Stubbs. In April 2000 they founded the Celtic Images Gallery in the beautiful surroundings of Hilton Court Gardens with its restaurants, crafts and landscaped grounds. They now display and sell the work of over twenty photographers all celebrating the beauty that is Pembrokeshire. The gallery can be contacted at: www.celticimages.co.uk

David Wilson seeks to capture the Pembrokeshire he has known and loved all his life. He photographs throughout the seasons, representing the county in all its moods, from the dramatic windswept beaches of mid-winter to gentle spring sunrises on the river. He is primarily a black and white photographer as it is his driving passion and Pembrokeshire lends itself perfectly to tonal interpretation. You can view more of his work at www.davidwilsonphotography.co.uk